Will the Real Me Please Stand Up!

Susan Davis

PACIFIC PRESS PUBLISHING ASSOCIATION
Mountain View, California
Oshawa, Ontario

Library of Congress Cataloging in Publication Data

Davis, Susan
  Will the Real Me Please Stand Up!

  (Redwood)
  1. Identification (Religion)   2. Christian Life
—Seventh-day Adventist authors.   I. Title.
BV4509.5.D29   248.4'8673   82-2142
ISBN 0-8l63-0479-3   AACR2

To my sister Maggie

Introduction

There's a poster with the caption, "I think I am who my friends think I am." Did you ever feel like that? I did. And that's just exactly the backward way to look at yourself. It takes most people a long time to figure out what they're really like, and sometimes what your friends think is more of a hindrance than a help!

We don't have a lot of time left now to discover who we are. Jesus is coming soon, and He's not going to take to heaven a lot of people who "think they are what their friends think they are." He's going to be taking a group of people who know themselves, because they know God.

Did you know that all wrapped up in the gift of eternal life is the gift of "knowing yourself"? It's one of the most fascinating gifts that Jesus gives us. And that's what this book is about.

May God bless you as you read it.

Susan Davis

Contents

Will the Real Me Please Stand Up!   11
The Original Man   14
Then Bad Things Started Happening   16
The Hole Inside   20
But I'm Different!   25
How Do I know Who I Am?   30
And What Is God Like?   34
What Are the Barriers?   37
It's a Scientific Experiment   39
Winning by Losing the Argument   44
A More Excellent Way   48
Let's Do It Right This Time   51
But What If I Do Something Dumb?   54
He Is the God of Time   56
Some People Have Already Tried It   60
The Gospel According to You—the Real You!   68
Catching the Picture   72
Promises for Personality Problems   77

Will the Real "You"
Please Stand Up?

Will the Real You Please Stand Up!

Will the real you please stand up
And tell the world the truth!
Let the real you come right out
And say that God is good!
Don't hide yourself behind a front,
Remember, God doesn't make junk!
Will the real you please stand up!

If you're hiding because you're hurt
Let Jesus make you whole;
Not the outside hurts alone He heals but
Hurts down in the soul.
Where things are bad, He'll make them good,
Bring joy for sadness, Oh, you really should
Let the real you please stand up!

God created, and it was good,
When everything was new.
God created something good
When He created you!
He likes your walk and He likes your smile,
He thinks you're special, 'Cause you're His child,
Let the real you please stand up!

Yes, the real me will now stand up
And tell the world the truth!
Yes, the real me will come right out
And say that God is good!
I won't hide myself behind a front,
I remember, God doesn't make junk!
Yes, the real me *will* stand up!

Susan Davis

Will the Real Me Please Stand Up!

There used to be a popular television program called "To Tell the Truth." It was made up of a panel of four members who tried to guess which one of the three guests on the show best fit the description read to them by the master of ceremonies. The description might read something like this:

"My name is Joe Smith. I am a logger from the state of Oregon. I work high in the mountains cutting virgin timber. My six sons and my wife help me, and we form a complete work crew. Part of my job is to top tall trees. I climb them, using a belt and strap-on boot spurs, and then saw off the tops. My wife is the cat skinner, and my sons do various other jobs, such as chasing and setting chokers, driving the log truck, felling, and bucking. The youngest son is camp cook. In this rather remote work spot, we sometimes have to deal with bears or other animals who are attracted by the smell of our food." The description might include a few more facts. As the emcee concluded his reading of the information, the three guests for the evening would walk on stage and take their seats.

Then came the exciting part! The panel members questioned the guests closely and tried to trap them into accidental slip-ups that would show whether they were ignorant of logging procedures. In thousands of homes, children and parents joined in. After a few minutes opinions would begin to form. In our home it went something like this:

Larry: "I guess the one on the left. He looks like he has some pretty well-developed muscles, and you'd have to, if you were a logger."

Kathy: "Oh, *him*! He's probably a lifeguard at Muscle Beach! *I* think it's the one on the right. He looks much more like a logger with that beard. And besides, he's wearing suspenders. Loggers always wear suspenders."

Before long, Dad, born and reared in a logging camp in Washington, would zero in. "It's that feller in the middle," he'd say quietly.

"What!" we would screech. "That little skinny man in the *suit*? It can't be!"

"You just wait," Dad would chuckle. "Under them fancy clothes is a man made outta pure wire and spring steel. Them heavy-muscled fellers ain't near the woodsmen these little wiry fellers is. And, why, anybody can put on a suit. I do it m'self ever' week."

"Quiet!" someone would hiss. "They're gonna tell!"

In the silence that crackled with excitement, the emcee would say, "All right the votes are in. Now, will the *real* . . . . Joe Smith . . . . *please* . . . . *stand up*!"

The man with the muscles would grate his chair a little, and Larry would start to say "Ah—." And when the bearded man leaned forward, Kathy would begin, "I thought—" And then the little, skinny man in the suit would stand up, accompanied in our home audience by Dad's quiet chuckle and some frustrated groans from three juniors!

"How did you know?" we'd harrass him afterwards. Then Dad would tell how a logger's eyes are always alert and moving, how he knew how to "set quiet" when he had to, and how he walked catlike and easy. Dad knew because he was experienced. He had eyesight we hadn't learned to use yet. Putting a suit on a logger wasn't any disguise at all to him!

"To Tell the Truth" isn't on the air anymore. But something very similar in real life is all around us. God has given each of us a true personality. But our friends may not know what it is. Sometimes we don't know ourselves. That's because Satan has been busy too. The enemy of goodness doesn't want our real, God-given personality to show—because that would glorify God. So he works as hard as he can to twist and distort it. And he puts up blocks and barriers and fences and hurdles to lock up that real personality inside us so tightly that it can't get out.

But God knows how to remove blocks and break down barriers and fences. He knows how to get around hurdles too. And He doesn't want your personality to go around in disguise, like a logger in a fancy suit. He wants it to come right out and glorify Him—especially right now at the end time of the world.

There probably isn't a person reading this book who hasn't thought in frustration to himself, "What am I anyway? And who am I? Will the Real Me please stand up!"

As you read on, you'll see how important it is to God, too, that you become just what He created you to be. In fact, He's the One who got you to thinking about it in the first place.

The Original Man

The first man had a perfect personality. He had no fears, doubts, or embarrassments, so he felt completely free just to be himself. And that was how God intended it to be. For the self that He had given Adam was designed to show the universe a little of what God is like. In time, God planned that there should be more of these new creatures and that each one of them would share a part of His personality. (It is so endlessly big that He couldn't give any one being all of it. But He gave each being a part.) And the purpose of each being was to keep that part right out front, where everyone else could see it.

The heavenly beings must have been excited and interested in all the goings-on in the brand-new world. Here was something special—a being very much like God, made in His image![1] How marvelous!

Perhaps because there had recently been a war in heaven and God's goodness had been challenged, He wanted to give the universal beings another proof of what He was really like. If He made creatures in His image and gave each of them a part of His own personality, then the other beings in the universe would know and understand Him better. So man's purpose right from the beginning was to glorify God—to help Him in the big argument that was going on between Himself and Satan about what God is really like.

Anything a person makes will reflect his personality. If three art students were to make three clay pots, they would, if they were all creative, end up with three different creations.

One pot might be small and delicate, with curved lines. You could guess that this person is a little shy and likes to be by himself more than in a crowd. He probably enjoys natural things and likes to work on small, detailed jobs rather than big, hard ones.

Another pot might be heavy and rather large. The person who made it would probably be a practical person. He doesn't want something just to look at; he wants something he can use. He would plan to use his pot for a planter or maybe a dog dish. Then it wouldn't have been a waste of time and effort. He likes things to be made sturdily, even if they don't look fancy.

The third pot might be modern, with clean flowing lines. It might have more than one use or be purely decorative. Its maker is a creative thinker and likes to think new thoughts and do new things.

Now if a clay pot can tell all that about its maker, what could a living godlike creature tell about *its* Maker? A lot! And Adam and Eve were doing a good job of it, naturally. They were being themselves, which meant they were giving a good picture of God to the universe.

Until they bit into the forbidden fruit.

1. Ellen G. White, "Purpose of Man's Creation," *Review and Herald,* February 11, 1902.

See also A. LeRoy Moore, *The Theology Crisis* (Corpus Christi, Texas: Life Seminars, Inc., 1980), pp. 70-72. Ellen G. White, *Education* (Mountain View, Calif.: Pacific Press Publishing Association, 1903), pp. 15-18.

Then Bad Things Started Happening

When Adam ate that bite of fruit, he didn't feel free to be himself anymore. He felt, instead, as if he needed to defend himself. So right away he tried to "get his act together." He "put up a front."

"Adam, where are you?" God called.

Hide, Adam. Don't let Him see you. He's out to get you! Strange thoughts came to the man who had so loved to fellowship with his Creator. Adam hid. He didn't answer. He didn't show his true self.

"Adam, where are you?" God called again, possibly standing right in front of the bush where Adam was hiding.

It's no use. He's seen me now. Well, I guess I'll have to answer. But I hope He doesn't ask any embarrassing questions—like where's my light robe? It was here a short time ago, but now it's gone. And these fig leaves are itchy. Come on, Eve. Don't act like that. He's right here in front of us. "I heard Your voice, God, and I was afraid. So I hid here, because my robe is gone. I sure feel strange, naked like this." Can't you sense how embarrassed and uncomfortable Adam and Eve must have felt? Even with the fig-leaf garments, they felt naked without the beautiful covering light that had always surrounded them.

"Who told you that you were naked?" God asked. "Did you eat of the tree in the middle of the garden?"

"This woman You made for me, Eve—she did it first." There. Now *he* was off the hook, and the blame was where it really belonged—on God and on Eve.

God looked at Eve. "What did you do?" He asked gently. He knew how frightened and strange they felt, and He tried to make things as easy as possible for them.

"It's the serpent's fault, really," Eve explained anxiously. "He lied to me."

So God cursed the serpent. But that didn't save Adam and Eve from the results of their choices. You know the rest of the story found in Genesis 3.

Adam and Eve had an advantage over us. At least they had the experience of being perfect for a while. But every person after Adam has been born with a sinful nature. It's true, we still have the original personalities God gave us, which should help show the universe a little more what He is like. But Satan begins work at birth, or even before, to try to destroy our individualities. And if God didn't give us His special protection, he would succeed.

Suppose God has given you beautiful teeth and an angel smile. Satan is sure to try to get you to stuff soda pop, candy, and other junk food into your mouth to insure early tooth decay and make you ashamed to use that smile. Satan loves to do things to us that will destroy God's image and embarrass Him before the universe. But worse than damaging our bodies is the damage he tries to do to our spirits.

Where Satan has been at work, you will see a girl born with a melodious, bubbling laugh, come out with a shrieky giggle of embarrassment. Or a naturally serious boy cracking corny jokes and guffawing loudly.

17

You'll see a naturally trusting person become a doubter, because Satan has caused others to lie to him. An honest child may turn sneaky. A loving one, rebellious.

It seems as if the more beautiful a person's God-given personality was meant to be, the more Satan tries to twist it. He sets up accidents and uses other people to hurt him. Satan tempts him to do bad things, which he will later feel guilty about. And guilt is one of the surest ways to tie up a good personality.

Sometimes by the time a person is ten or twelve years old, the enemy has already put up such high walls of fear, anger, doubt, hatred, or rebellion around his true self, that no one knows what he would be like if he were relaxed and feeling comfortable with himself. And God mourns, because the special gifts He has given that boy or girl are hidden behind ugly characteristics. That's an insult to Him.

But God always has a counterattack. He doesn't let Satan get away with that kind of sabotage without doing something about it. God sent His Son down to this earth to live a perfect life, as Adam should have. That showed His goodness. Then God's Son paid the price for our disobedience by dying for us. That showed His love. And with these two weapons, His *goodness* and His *love,* He fights for us against the enemy of souls. If God can persuade a person to *choose His way*, He will take charge of that person. He will actually live in his mind, directing him in all the activities of his life. And when He comes in, He brings with Him eternal life. John tells us, "He who has the Son has life. . . . I write this to you who believe in the name of the Son of God, that you may know that you have eternal life." "He who was born of God [Jesus] keeps him, and the evil one does not touch him." 1 John 5:12, 13, 18, RSV.

How would you like to live forever? Forever frightened. Forever angry. Forever upset. Forever hurt. Wouldn't that be the most miserable eternal life you can think of? So when God comes in, His Spirit begins to undo the work that Satan has done in our lives. Remember, most of this happens *after* we choose Jesus as our Lord. Some people think they have to improve *before* they can come to Jesus. That's Satan's last-ditch effort to keep them away from Him, because, of course, they can't improve very much until He comes into the lives of the ones who need help.

Jesus is willing to take us just the way we are. One of the most important things a person can know is that he'll never "get it all together" until he fills up the empty place inside—the empty place that exists in a life when Jesus isn't there.

The Hole Inside

All God's creatures are dependent. That means they can't live without His life flowing to them every minute of every hour of every day. The animals can't, the plants can't, the people can't. But there is a difference between human beings and the lower forms of life. When God made the higher kinds of beings— angels and the new creatures called man—He wanted more than obedience. He wanted voluntary love. He wanted man to obey because he loved God, not because he couldn't do anything else. And to get voluntary love and obedience, God had to make man with the power to choose between right and wrong.

There is no comparison, to God, between a daisy or a squirrel and a human person made in His own image. The daisy and the squirrel always do as commanded. Any perversion in their behavior is the result of sin.

For instance, God programmed the daisy to grow *up*. So the daisy grows up. And God told the squirrel, "Eat nuts, berries, seeds." So that is what the squirrel eats. And you do not even see a squirrel trying to invent a soufflé that will make the nuts taste better! He does not whine, "I hate nuts. Why can't I eat algae, like the fish? Why can't I drink nectar, like the hummingbird?'' No. If you were to lay out a plate of the most delicious algae, a glass of the sweetest nectar, and a dish of choice nuts and berries, the squirrel would go for the nuts and berries every time. *Even if nobody was watching!* He doesn't want anything else.

As you may have noticed, this is not usually the way man acts. God said, ''Behold, I have given you every plant yielding seed . . . and every tree with seed in its fruit; you shall have them for food.'' Genesis 1:29, RSV. Later, He added ''the herb of the field'' (Genesis 3:18) to the diet He wanted man to have. And later still, He permitted certain meats and other animal products, such as eggs and milk, to be used. See Genesis 9:3. But instead of being content with all this variety, man chose to invent ham casserole and shrimp cocktail. *Man can choose.*

Now occasionally, we do see a man or woman who chooses the way God planned for him. Daniel was that kind. When he was offered ham casserole, or whatever it was the king of Babylon had on his table, Daniel said, ''No, thanks. I eat fruits, grains, and nuts.''

Man can choose.

When a man does choose, as Daniel did, to obey God, there is nothing that brings God greater joy! We are told that God is so happy when one of His children returns love and obedience to Him that He rejoices over him with singing.[1]

Not only was man made to be dependent on God, but he was also made to be God's dwelling place.[2] Of course, if a man does not choose to obey, God cannot dwell in him. This leaves man with a vacancy.

This question appeared in the ''ASKen (ASK Ken) column of the February, 1981 issue of the *Signs of the Times* magazine.

''I feel like a mannequin. Everything is put together perfectly on the outside, but I'm hollow inside—noth-

21

ing there. I read the Bible a lot. I believe Jesus is coming soon. But inside I'm still empty. Why? I want to be filled."

Ken McFarland, who writes this column, answered the letter this way:

"Take that Bible you've been reading and look up 1 Corinthians 6:19, 20. Do you see where these verses say you are God's temple?

"Just as a house with no one living in it is empty, a temple without God living in it is empty too.

"You want to be filled. Then ask Christ to come into the temple of your heart as your permanent Guest, . . . and you will be able to join Paul in saying that 'Christ liveth in me.' Galatians 2:20."

Inside each of us is a funny kind of longing, craving, empty feeling. Man was made to be filled with something.

Now the last thing Satan wants for man to be filled with is the Holy Spirit of God. So he will use all his power to get man off the track.

"Fill up with money," he'll urge. "Nice gold, silver, even paper dollars. Start a bank account. Buy a beautiful house, fancy furniture, pretty clothes. *Then* you'll feel good about yourself."

And some people believe that. All their lives they try to satisfy themselves with the things that money can buy. Money becomes a kind of god to them. It seems to have so much power to get things they want. But money cannot fill the God-shaped hole inside the body-temple.

"Fill up with good feelings," the enemy whispers to some. "Try a little marijuana. Like that? How about some heroin? Ah-h-h! That's even better! Feel the rush? Now you're ready for the ultimate experience—LSD. This will really turn you on, and you'll be as a god."

Maybe you know someone who has tried to fill his body-temple with good feelings. All such attempts end with failure.

Six thousand years ago, Adam and Eve proved that food is no substitute for God's Spirit. Yet, today, many people still try to make food a god. Food can fill the body, but it can never fill the soul.

If a person tries to fill the empty place inside with *anything*—money, drugs, food, sex, education, even happiness—*anything* but the Spirit of God, he is actually choosing Satan for his ruler. Satan isn't really a god, but he claims to be one. And he does have the power to enter a human body-temple and become its ruler. He has the advantage of being able to force his way in, too. That is something the true God will never do. He waits for His creatures to choose, for then He is assured of true love and loyalty. And the person who chooses Him becomes a complete person, at rest inside himself.

Satan's way, in contrast, is to push in and take over whenever possible. He will hold on until he is forced out by a Higher Power. While he is the ruling spirit in a person's life, he does everything possible to destroy the true personality of that individual. That is how he "gets back" at God.

A young woman became a Christian after she was already married. Her husband did not like her new beliefs and tried to get her to give them up. But she would not. So one day he decided to "get even" with her. He waited until she was away, and then went through the house with an ax. He broke every piece of furniture, every picture, every lamp. He went into the kitchen and threw all the dishes out of the cupboard against the wall, until nothing was left but shattered china on the floor. He completely destroyed everything the poor wife had worked so hard to help buy and kept so neatly. When the woman came home, she went into shock! It didn't look like the same house she had left a few hours before.

But the man's plan didn't work so well. For when the rage had passed, he realized that *he* did not have any furniture anymore, either. Nor did *he* have any dishes to eat from. In fact, he didn't have a wife, either. She left. And he ended up sitting in his broken-up home in despair.

That's something like what is happening with Satan. There's no question that he's making an awful mess of things down here. But every time he does something bad to one of God's children, he is only piling up more punishment for himself. And when Satan gets too hard on a person, that man or woman or child may appeal to God for help. Then Satan loses him. In the end, the devil will be found sitting in his broken-up world waiting for the judgment fires to destroy him for his evil work.

And for us, even for those of us whose personalities have been beaten and broken by Satan's cruelty, Jesus has provided a new life. We don't have to wait for it. It can begin right now. He has made it possible again to be everything He created us to be. If we choose Him as the ruling Spirit in our body-temples, He'll do the work of building us back together whole and sound inside so that the Real Me can stand up.

1. Ellen G. White, *The Desire of Ages* (Mountain View, Calif.: Pacific Press Publishing Association, 1940), p. 834.

2. *Ibid.*, p. 161.

Also see LeRoy Moore, pp. 84-87.

But I'm Different!

Sooner or later, everyone thinks it. If you're a teen-ager, maybe you've already complained to your mom or dad, "How come I'm so different from the other kids?" Maybe you've even shed a few tears about it. Well-meaning grown-ups will say, "Why, don't be silly. You're no different than I was at your age." But that doesn't help at all, because you know deep down that it's not true. You *are* different. Inside especially. But even outside.

One look in the bathroom mirror will tell you that your hair is too (thick, thin, straight, curly, light, dark, long, short, dull—circle the ones that fit!). And if you should happen to see yourself in a full-length mirror, you will immediately notice that you are also too (fat, thin, short, tall, bumpy, straight, stooped, squashed-together, strung-out—circle the ones that apply!). And worst of all is that peculiar smile. You may wonder how your friends can stand to be around you when you're happy!

Did you know that many people are embarrassed about their smiles? That is my observation, at least. One woman I know has the most gorgeous smile I have seen, with perfect, beautiful, white teeth. One day I said, "Mary, you have the prettiest smile. I love it!"

25

And do you know what she did? She covered her mouth up quickly with her hand and said, "Oh, I don't know how you can say that! I am ashamed when I see my smile in a mirror, because I've always thought my smile looked so terrible!"

Guess who had been working on her?

Satan knows that you are different—all too well! He sees that special bit of heavenly spark that Jesus gave *you* and *no one else* in the history of this world. And the devil grinds his teeth in rage to think that if he doesn't get to work and do something fast, this part of God's personality will soon be reflecting God to the world. So he attacks.

Now sometimes Satan "steps on his own tail," so to speak. And this is one of the times he does it. If he wouldn't get so concerned about your unique personality, you might never discover the special points that make you different. So he tries to direct your attention away from the fact that God made your personality unique—and he attacks your perception of your physical appearance. "You're different," he hisses, flooding you with embarrassment at the thought. "Look at the way your mouth curls up on one side. No one else's mouth is that way. How strange you are, with your thick waist and big feet. Regular people don't look like you. If I were you, I'd crawl in a hole and hide somewhere." He makes us feel as if being different is something awful, something bad, the worst thing that could possibly happen to us.

But he's wrong! *Being different is good!* It's fantastic! It's the best thing that could've ever happened to anyone! If we would only recognize that the embarrassment and frustration are not the feelings God created us to have, but are suggested by Satan. He's angry that God did it again—created *another* wonderful man-creature, different from any other that has been created so far. And, oh no! this creature is reflecting the goodness of God.

Often he tries to make us unhappy about how we look. If he can do that, it's likely we won't act out our true, good feelings. And also it's easier to get us to try to look like everyone else. An impossible task, of course.

But who hasn't seen a willowy girl trying to look classy in a straight skirt and tight sweater? Or the chunky, athletic one attempting to be feminine in a ruffled, tiered skirt and lace blouse? If you were to ask each of them why she dressed that way, very likely the answer would be, "It's the *style*. And I don't want to be out of style and look different from everyone else!"

Boys are just as susceptible. If one brand of jeans becomes popular or one type of haircut, soon nearly every male in school will be sporting it.

Sounds as if we're embarrassed about being ourselves, doesn't it? Never listen to Satan when he tries to get you feeling that way—*never!* If the thought comes to your mind that you're different and are really an exception to the human race, just say, "You'd better believe it! Praise the Lord!" Say it now, in fact, just for practice. Say, "I'm unique. Wasn't God good to make me special this way? Praise the Lord! There's no one exactly like me!"

When I was ten or twelve years old, or maybe a little older, I had a problem about feeling "different." I asked my mother what to do, and she said, "Look to God. God has all the answers." So I looked to God. Only I was so hung up about being different that I even got mixed up about what God is like!

It seemed to me that if I could just get myself looking right on the outside, then people would like me, and I would be "OK." That is, of course, the opposite of how it works! I didn't realize that I was OK to begin with, because, as the saying goes, "God doesn't make junk."

So when I looked to God to try to find out what He was like, I looked at Him on the outside too. I read a description of Jesus written by a woman who had seen Him in vision—Ellen G. White. And in this description she said that Jesus has long, white, curly hair, resting on His shoulders.—*Early Writings*, page 16.

I became very embarrassed for Jesus! Long hair on men wasn't in style then. I hoped not too many people would read this part of the book!

Then in Revelation 1:13 I read how Jesus walked among the seven golden candlesticks "girt about the paps with a golden girdle." That really shook me— even after I found out that in that old-fashioned King James English, it only meant He wore a gold belt around His chest.

I didn't understand till I was much older that the things prophets see in visions are not always exactly what they appear. But the things seen in visions always *mean something*. Daniel saw Rome, a nation, as a huge, ugly beast with iron teeth. No one in Rome ever looked the least like Daniel's beast! But God was showing the character of Rome. The Roman soldiers were cruel, and Roman emperors wicked.

So when John saw Jesus the way he did in his vision, it doesn't necessarily mean Jesus looks or dresses just that way. Perhaps, since Paul calls truth a girdle (belt) and since John saw a belt around Jesus' chest, it may mean simply that truth is precious to Jesus, that truth is at the heart of His character.

Years before John's vision, Moses had asked to see God, and God consented. He hid Moses in a crack in a big rock, put His hand over him, and went by with His back to Moses. And Moses records what God "looks" like—"merciful and gracious, longsuffering, and abun-

28

dant in goodness and truth." See Exodus 33:18-23 and 34:5-8. And that's what God wants us to see about Him—His character. Looking at Jesus from the outside doesn't help us at all. It didn't help the Jews in Jesus' day, for as Isaiah had told them years before, "there is no beauty that we should desire him." Isaiah 53:2.

And it didn't help me, either. In fact, in addition to being upset about how different I was, I now had another problem. God was even more different from me!

If I had only known it, I was just one hairbreadth away from a great big, beautiful piece of truth. Jesus *is* more different from you or me than we can ever know. Not just because He has long, curly, white hair or may wear a gold belt around His chest. But because *His personality includes all other personalities!*

So now you know where to find yours!

How Do I Know Who I Am?

Even though knowing God is the ultimate key to knowing yourself, it helps to know the different types of human personalities God has made. For in finding out about people, we are also finding out something about the God who made people.

Most persons are combinations of four basic personality types (adapted from Tim LaHaye's books, primarily *Transformed Temperaments*). I call them Happy, Leader, Feeler, and Cool Sam. Satan has found different ways to tempt each type of personality. So as you read the weaknesses of each, you will see how cleverly he works against God. As you read, see if you can tell which of these descriptions is most like yourself.

Type one is the happy-go-lucky kind of person. He usually sees the cheerful side of life and loves to joke and make people laugh. Happy is a fun person to have around. He is loveable. He makes a party a party. In fact, he can almost be a party himself. He likes all kinds of people too. And they nearly always like him. Because Happy has such a pleasant way about him, Satan tries to offset his cheerful influence by giving him some annoying habits. He makes promises easily, but too often fails to keep them. He forgets the chores or errands he was supposed to do. Important things don't seem as important to Happy as they might really be. He is likely to be overweight, because he likes to do things that feel good, and eating is one of them. He's not very neat, either. Happy likes to talk a lot. If there are any empty places in the conversation, Happy will fill them in—even if he can't think of the right thing to say. That means that often he puts his foot in his mouth! He needs to learn to listen more carefully and talk less. But Happy likes to please people, so he tries to be good. He cries easily over his mistakes, but soon forgets how bad he felt. If he doesn't let Jesus come in and work in his life, Happy will end up living a carefree and useless existence, never making much of his gifts and talents.

Type two is a Leader. Leader seems to have endless energy. He likes to be out on the football field or the track or in the gym. Leader will hold his own opinion even if it's different from everyone else's. He does not care much what others think about him. He just charges along toward his goal, and very often he reaches it simply because he just won't quit! However, in the course of going where he wants to go, it is easy for Leader to step on people's feelings and never realize it. He tends to say what he thinks, never intending to crush feelings the way he does. Leader isn't very neat, either. He needs a housekeeper or a secretary to do all his detail work for him! Leader has so many good qualities and so much persistence that it is hard for him to follow God's way. It seems to him as if he can try harder and be better on his own. But when he is convinced that he needs Jesus, he becomes an energetic worker for God.

Type three I call Feeler. Feeler is very emotional. He loves music, art, and books. He can look at a spider web and see beautiful things in it, whereas

Leader would only see a bothersome mess of sticky strings. Feeler can be a good student, but he doesn't care to be in large crowds of people for a long time. He may go to a party where he will watch Happy and listen to Leader, but he himself will probably be rather quiet. However, if Feeler finds another person similar to himself, he can talk for long periods and hardly realize where the time has gone. Feeler thinks often of how he feels, and if he loves Jesus, he will understand better than some how Jesus feels. Feeler may choose to be a writer, an artist, a musician, an interior decorator, or a missionary. He may do anything which helps him express his deep feelings or will help another person. Helping others is one of his best qualities. Feeler is usually very neat, also. But because he feels so much, he is often a fearful person. He may think too long about bad things, then get depressed. He needs to learn the text of Philippians 4:8. "Whatsoever things are true, whatsoever things are honest, whatsoever things are just, whatsoever things are pure, whatsoever things are lovely, whatsoever things are of good report . . . think on these things." If Feeler gives his life to God, the Holy Spirit will work to take away his fearfulness and give him pleasant things to think about. Then he will become a hopeful, encouraging, loving person.

Type four is a rather self-possesed personality. I call him Cool Sam. In case of emergency, Happy will go all to pieces and probably say just the wrong thing. Leader will try to make people do what he sees as the best solution to the problem. Feeler will feel sad and will be very sympathetic with any victims. But Cool Sam will probably calm everyone with a few quiet words and think of just the right thing to do. He doesn't panic. On the other hand, Cool Sam doesn't like to show his good feelings very often, either. If he likes someone very much, he may think of all the nice things he would like to do or say to that person, but he probably will not do or say them. He will go through all the agonies of Charlie Brown over the little red-haired girl. He is afraid someone would make fun of him. Cool Sam may be very talented, but unless he lets Jesus into his life, he will be too afraid to do anything with his talent. He doesn't like to try new things, either. Often he gives up before he starts, just by saying "I can't." Cool Sam likes to be neat, but he often moves so slowly that his jobs take a long time to get done. He tends to look down on those who are not as organized as himself. Cool Sam needs to let Jesus make him a warmer and more forgiving person. Once he gets started on something good, like serving the Lord, he will go all the way.

Each of us is a combination of two or more of these types of temperaments. Each has strengths and weaknesses. Looking at your personality could be a very discouraging thing if you didn't know that Jesus could do something about the weak parts. But when you choose Him to be the ruler of your body-temple, He begins right away to make the weak places strong. After a while, it becomes more difficult to tell what type of temperament he began with, because Jesus has done so much work that the personality has become a more balanced blend of all four kinds.

Many of the changes that come as a result of our being a Christian happen slowly and quietly. They take place when we begin to study what Jesus is like. He had all the good parts of all the kinds of personalities and none of the bad parts. So everybody can find something about Jesus that he understands. And from there, we can go on to the parts we don't understand yet. Jesus brings the understanding with Him when He comes into our lives.

And What Is God Like?

A Happy person can find something about God that he understands right in Genesis 1. Verse 31 says, "God saw every thing that he had made, and, behold, it was very good." He was happy with it. He liked what He had done. Not only that, but God wanted someone like Himself around. That's why He made Adam and Eve. He liked to talk too. We have a record of His visiting Adam and Eve every evening, in the cool of the day.

And many years later, when Jesus came to Earth to show us what God is like, we read how He spent days and days healing people, talking to them, visiting them. Jesus likes all kinds of people. That was one thing that bothered the Pharisees. They noticed that He was talking with some whom they considered sinners. And they observed that He was eating too. Not fasting, as they thought He should have done. A Happy kind of person can definitely see how Jesus is like himself. Many sought Him out, because He was nice to have around. He was invited to weddings and feasts, and He went and enjoyed them.

A Leader can see an aspect of Jesus in himself too. When Israel was coming out of Egypt, Jesus Himself (as the preexistent Son of God) led them in the cloud by day and the pillar of fire by night. Earthly kings were afraid of His leadership ability. He was so mighty that He never lost a battle. When the people followed

Him, they were winners. Centuries later when He came to Earth, His disciples followed Him. He seemed to have something about Him that made even the Pharisees and Sadducees keep coming back. The thing a Leader might find hard to understand about Jesus is why He suddenly stopped leading and let Himself be led away to die on the cross.

Feeler can understand that much better, because he has often felt deeply for other people. When he sees someone in need, Feeler would give the coat off his back to help. He can see that Jesus is like himself when He spent hours and hours on His feet helping the crowds who came to Him for healing and counsel and when He died for sinful man.

Cool Sam sees himself in Jesus when he reads how Jesus quieted the storm with a few words. He admires Jesus' standing calmly in the Garden of Gethsemane and remembering to ask that the disciples be allowed to go, since the mob was not after them. Cool Sam knows how Jesus might have felt before the angry crowd, saying and doing just the right thing.

When we see Jesus in aspects of ourselves, we feel more sure of what we're really like. And the more we study about Jesus, the more we discover about ourselves. The strange thing is that the better we know ourselves, the less we think about ourselves. It's really more interesting to look at a perfect photograph than one that is out of focus, isn't it? See 2 Corinthians 3:18.

As our interest in God grows, we begin to see Him in nature too. We see His beauty in the flowers, His sense of humor in kittens and monkeys. We find Him to be a practical, realistic God when we look at and walk on a piece of bedrock on a hillside. As we notice these things about God, one day we realize that He is really, truly our Friend and that somewhere along the way to knowing Him, we have walked into eternal life.

For John tells us, "This is life eternal, that they might know thee the only true God." John 17:3.

And knowing Him makes it easier to work with Him as He works on our minds and hearts.

What Are the Barriers?

Earlier we spoke of barriers, fences, walls, and hurdles that Satan puts up around our personalities. Of course, these aren't literal fences and walls. You can't feel the wood and brick of them with your hands. But they're there, nonetheless. And you can feel them in other ways.

The barriers we are talking about are negative qualities that keep us from doing or saying what we might really want to. The barriers are fear, guilt, rebellion, hatred, anger—things like that. Even hurts from the past can be a barrier that will block the acting out of our real selves. Charlie Brown never does deliver the note to the little red-haired girl because he has a fear barrier. He's afraid people will laugh at him, as they have in the past.

In the Bible, we read the story of the prodigal son. When he wanted to return to his father after wasting his inheritance, his guilt kept him from returning as a son. He felt he was so wicked that he must return as a servant. But the forgiving father saw beyond the barrier of his son's guilt. He knew that his son really desired to have things the way they had been before. He wanted to be a son, not a servant. The forgiving father pushed the guilt aside, wrapped his arms around the boy, and called him "my son."

This is how Jesus helps break down our barriers. He looks for our true feelings and does everything He can to encourage them. His understanding and goodness help melt our fear, anger, guilt, and rebellion. Without Jesus, we would be forever trapped behind barriers, never free to be ourselves. But when Jesus was here, He did what we aren't able to do. He worked through all the barriers Satan tried to impose on Him.

When He might have been angry, He wasn't.

When He might have rebelled, He submitted.

When He might have been afraid, He went ahead bravely—acting out His real personality in spite of what people thought.

When it was time for Him to die, He did a tremendous thing. He took upon Himself every wrong thing everyone else has ever done and took the punishment for them. In doing this, He bought the right for us to be free. He will give that freedom to anyone who asks.

When a person asks for forgiveness, he is freed from the barrier of guilt. When he asks for Christ's love, he is freed from hatred. When he asks for the power of the Holy Spirit to live in him, he is freed from fear. And so on, down the list. The barriers come down when Jesus comes in. He'll work through the fear, the anger, the hurts, the guilt, the rebellion the same way He did when He was here on earth. Only this time, He's doing it in *you*—so the Real You can stand up.

It's a Scientific Experiment

As God begins to do His rebuilding work in our lives, He expects us to work along with Him. It's hard for God to do much with us if we complain about the way He does things. God will only do as much as we *let Him* do. The Bible tells us to "let." "Let this mind be in you, which was also in Christ Jesus." Philippians 2:5. It stands to reason that when Jesus' mind is in us, we act like Jesus, talk like Jesus, and think like Jesus. That is what He is asking us to do—not by trying, but by *letting His mind be in us*.

WE	HE
Choose Him	Becomes the Ruling Spirit
Give Him permission to work	Does the changing
Obey Him	Gives us the power to obey.

There are two ways for a Christian to get into trouble. One is *not letting Jesus work*. The other is *trying to do His part of the job*.

People get into long discussions about which is more important—"faith" (believing in Jesus) or "works" (obeying Jesus). The real issue is not which is more important, but *which comes first*.

Faith must come first. "Without faith it is impossible to please him." Hebrews 11:6.

Works, or obedience, comes next. It's important too. If we don't obey the Ten Commandments, no one will see any difference between the Christians and non-Christians. Right? *What we do will show to others the love of Jesus that is already in us because we believe*.

As we believe and choose to obey God, He begins to change things in our lives. And because God is a God of order, He does these things for us in a planned way. If we know the science of rebuilding the personality, the work can go much faster.

One of the most important things to know about how God works is this: *Nothing works by feeling*.

We're studying a *science*. If you were experimenting with the science of chemistry, you would certainly not base your experiments on feelings. If you were about to combine two parts of hydrogen gas with one part of oxygen gas, you might get the feeling it would turn into orange juice. But it wouldn't! It would turn into water. To get orange juice, you would have to mix an orange with a juicer! (I'm teasing!) But one thing is sure. You'll never, never, never get orange juice when you mix two parts of hydrogen gas with one part of oxygen gas—no matter *how* you feel! Under the appropriate conditions you will always, always, always get water. It's a scientific rule. So God has a similar kind of rule for working inside people as He has for working chemistry. And how you feel has nothing to do with whether the rules work. If you mix God's promises and your faith, you will get results. Always, always, always.

1 Promise + 1 Believer = Results.

Another important thing to know is this: *You have to follow the directions*.

They're simple. You can follow them as you read, right now. The directions are the same for every promise you need to claim.

1. Choose Jesus to be the ruling Spirit in your body-temple. Tell Satan to go away.

2. Tell Jesus you choose to follow His rules. If you choose, He will make it possible. He doesn't expect you to obey without His help.

3. Forgive everyone who did anything bad to you. And forgive yourself too.

4. Start talking to Jesus and listening to Him every day. That means reading the Bible (His words), praying, and listening for Jesus to speak to your mind. Some people call this kind of communication a "thought voice."

When you've done these four things, you're ready to start helping Jesus work inside you. The Bible tells us that we actually share Jesus' mind and personality when we claim His promises. 2 Peter 1:4.

Do you know what a claim check is? I took a shoe to be repaired recently, and the repairman gave me a claim check. "Now be sure to bring the claim check when you come to get your shoe," he told me. "Because I have so many shoes in here, it would take me an hour to open up every bag and try to find yours. So I make it a policy not to give back a shoe unless the claim check is returned." You can be sure I took very good care of that little numbered card he gave me!

The promises in the Bible work like a claim check. They don't do anything for us unless we present them to the Father, in the name of Jesus, and say, "I want this, please." I could've carried that claim check for my shoe in my purse for a hundred years and taken very good care of it. But it would not have done me any good as far as getting my shoe back unless I presented it to the repairman.

My grandmother was a very devout woman and had great respect for the Bible. She put it on a beautifully crocheted doily and dusted the Book faithfully. But she never opened it and read it! Her church taught that only the priest could understand God's Word. So she never knew about many of the promises inside. And she never got to know God as well as she might have.

We know better. We know that the Bible is meant to be used. It is God's bank account for our spirits, and in it He has given us thousands of "promise checks." All we have to do to get the promises is to "cash the check"! Here's how to do it.

1. Find a promise that will take care of your problem.

2. Ask God to give you whatever was promised.

3. Believe that God will do it.

4. Thank Him for doing it.

God isn't asking you to do something unreasonable. When you cash a check at the bank, you have to do just about the same things. You go to the counter inside the bank, and you say, "I'd like to cash this check, please." You *have* the check, and now you're *asking*. And the teller says, "All right, please sign it on the back."

Signing it shows you believe the check is good. You don't say, "Well, I don't know if I want to sign it or not. What if the person who wrote the check changes his mind? Then I will have signed it for nothing." The teller would think you were slightly confused. So you sign the check and give it to the teller, showing that you believe she will follow through and give you the money in return. Then, if you're polite, as your mom taught you to be, you say "Thank you" as the teller gives you the money.

The difference in cashing in a promise is that you trust God completely to send the answer when He

42

wants to and how He wants to. And you always thank Him first, because you know He is going to do it for you. For every promise in the Bible is guaranteed by God and will do everything it says it will do, according to God's will for your life.

It helps to get your promise checks together and organized. On pages 77-79 are listed some of the promises and directions that will help you break down any fences Satan has tried to build around your Real Self. If the promise you need isn't listed, there are about 3500 more in the Bible. As you read it day by day, you will find them yourself. A promise is any verse that offers to give you something. "Great peace have they which love thy law: and nothing shall offend them" (Psalm 119:165), is a promise that offers us peace (if we love God's law) and protection from hurt feelings.

Remember to follow the rules exactly when you claim a promise, because this is a scientific experiment. And remember, it doesn't matter how you feel when you ask. If you're following the directions, God will do the rest. Even if you feel awful.

Winning by Losing the Argument

Few of us have trouble recognizing and accepting our good qualities, even if they've been buried up till now. In fact, just knowing that you really *are* cheerful or loving or artistic or self-sacrificing seems to be about all it takes to encourage those good traits to show themselves. "And ye shall know the truth, and the truth shall make you free." John 8:32.

But what about the bad things? What if you realize that you are also the type that cries over the tiniest little incidents? Or have a bad temper? Or are fearful? It almost seems as if it would be better to just sort of forget about those things and try not to let them show. "Use a little self-control!" Has anyone ever told you that?

Self-control is a good thing, no doubt about it. But there's something that can top it—God-control. When you choose Jesus for the ruling Spirit in your body-temple, God-control is available to you. Here is how it works.

Instead of trying to cover up or ignore your bad points, admit them to Jesus. Suppose you have a hard time telling the truth. Tell Jesus, "I lie. I can't stop." In fact, right now, pick a fault that troubles you and tell God about it. Say, "I'm afraid. I can't control my fears." Or, "I have a bad temper. I get angry all the time." Name *your* problem, whatever it is. If you're alone right now, *do it out loud*.

Are you brave enough?

All right, here's a quiet space to do it:

How did you feel? Embarrassed? But maybe kind of strong too? Really, it does take a brave person to say the truth even when it hurts. *Saying it to Jesus is the first step*. It shows that you're willing to be honest with yourself and with God. You may have had a very bad fault to confess, but at this point, God is actually pleased with you for telling Him about it.

The next thing to do is to find out what God thinks about this fault. From the Bible, if you can. The Ten Commandments (Exodus 20:3-17) are pretty clear on most points, but you will find a lot of God's thinking about sin in Proverbs too. So if you don't know your Bible well yet, try those two places first.

Suppose your fault is lying. The text of Proverbs 12:22 says, "Lying lips are abomination to the Lord." Now you know what God thinks of lying. And what God thinks is true. *That's the second thing to do–find out what God thinks*.

The third step often begins like this:

"But lying isn't the worst sin. Not as bad as stealing. for instance."

"Lying lips are abomination to the Lord."

"I don't lie very often, anyway. Not nearly as much as Tom Forney."

"Lying lips are abomination to the Lord."

"When it's really important to tell the truth, I usually come across with it."

"LYING LIPS ARE ABOMINATION TO THE LORD!"

What's happening is that you're arguing with the Holy Spirit. And it is actually possible to win the argument too. When you do, it's called "the unpardonable sin." The Holy Spirit says, "OK. You win." And He quits making you uncomfortable about your sins. Then you will not feel as if you need to ask God to forgive them. And if you don't ask God to forgive them, they cannot be forgiven. That's why they are "unpardonable." But any sin you *do* ask God to forgive, *He will forgive*. So the safest thing to do is to let the Holy Spirit win the argument, and you agree with God that lying lips are abomination to the Lord. Because He can't do another thing for you until you do.

So say right now, "All right, God. Lying lips are abomination to the Lord. I have lying lips. I choose to be honest about it. Now *please*"—Did you guess the rest of Step 3?—"HELP ME!"

Now, quickly, find a promise that has what you need. A few verses up the page—Proverbs 12:19. "The lip of truth shall be established for ever." That's great! Ask God for it! The "lip of truth" can be yours. Give God control of your mouth, and He'll make sure that what comes out of it is good, true, pure, honest.

So we have four steps to go through when we are trying to overcome our faults or strengthen our weak points.

1. Face the truth. Admit it out loud, if possible, to God and to yourself.

2. Find out from the Bible what God thinks about the fault. Read it out loud.

3. Agree with God, out loud. Ask for help.

4. Find a promise that has what you need, and let God take control.

When you speak out loud to God, it seems more real, because your ears can hear it. When you only think something, it's very easy to forget what you thought or to say later, "Nothing really happened."

As God takes control, you can be sure He'll be as easy on you as possible. You have to learn, and He is teaching you a better way to be.

A More Excellent Way

"Won't you please play your trumpet for church, Don?" the woman asked one morning after Sabbath services.

"*Me*?" Don said, feeling a sudden attack of weak knees. "Oh, I—uh—I don't think so."

"Oh, come on, Don," the woman continued with sweet persistence. "I know you're a good trumpeter. Didn't you used to play with a jazz band before your conversion?"

"Yes, but that was *different*," Don tried to explain.

"Surely you could play us a simple hymn," she went on.

"No, no, I just can't do it," Don said firmly.

"*Now, Don*" his conscience began, after the woman had left. "*Anyone who can play 'Twelfth Street Rag' can play 'Fairest Lord Jesus.'*"

"It's not that I can't play it, but I can't play it in front of all those—saints! And a whole churchful of them! I can't do that!"

"*Don, you used to play while hundreds of people danced,*" his conscience continued.

"Yes," Don argued back. "But I was up there with five other guys. And the dancers weren't looking at me; they were looking at each other. And I've never played a hymn on the trumpet. I've never played anything but jazz."

"You have a hymnbook, Don. You could learn."

So Don learned a hymn. It wasn't too hard because he was skilled on his instrument. He still wasn't brave enough to volunteer.

The woman in charge of music was rather persistent, however, and a few weeks later, she tried again.

"Don, won't you play your trumpet for church?" she asked one Sabbath morning.

"I—well—I don't think I can do that," Don answered.

But she caught the hesitation in his voice. "Why? Don't you know any hymns?"

Now he was caught. "Yes, I do know a hymn," he admitted. And then it came out. "I just don't know if I would have the nerve to play with all those people watching me."

Aha, thought the music coordinator. He's shy. Aloud she said, "Why, Don, that can be easily gotten around. We'll just have you stand in the baptistry with the curtains shut. You can play in seclusion. In fact, I think it would give a very good effect."

The woman was so enthusiastic that Don finally gave in. He played his first solo from the baptistry with the curtains drawn. Not being able to see his audience, he could relax. After a few specials from the closed baptistry, he got brave enough to stand in a place where people could see him, but still not directly in front. And finally, the love and appreciation of the church members broke down his fears. He was able to stand in front, face the congregation, and play for the Lord.

God wants us to develop our talents and use them for Him, but He doesn't push us onstage, shaking and fearful the first time, and say, "Look! I'm expecting you to be perfect! Now!" He works the easiest way possible for us to accept. He'll let us stand behind the curtain for a while, until we're brave enough to come out.

The Bible tells us that when the Israelites moved into Canaan, the Lord drove the wicked inhabitants out of the land "by little and little." Exodus 23:30. And often that's how He drives out our personal enemies of fear, doubt, anger, laziness, forgetfulness, and all the rest—"by little and little." And as those enemies are overcome, our talents and strengths are released, as Don's were.

Paul says, "Where the Spirit of the Lord is, there is liberty. But we all . . . beholding . . . the glory of the Lord, are changed into the same image from glory to glory." 2 Corinthians 3:17, 18.

Little by little, from glory to glory, the Real Me stands up!

Let's Do It Right This Time

It's a fact that if a person learned to do something the wrong way before he knew Jesus very well, he will have to unlearn that wrong way and learn the correct way.

Take Peter, for example. Although he had been with Jesus for three years and must have known that Jesus didn't use weapons, what did Peter bring to the Garden of Gethsemane? A sword! And what did he do with it when the soldiers attacked? Right. He cut off the ear of the high priest's servant. And he was probably aiming for his neck. So Peter had to unlearn fighting and learn fighting of a different kind. God has a sword too. It's called the sword of the Spirit. But He doesn't cut off people's heads with it. He goes for the heart—but in love. Peter had to learn that way of fighting. And he did. When the Spirit of the Lord came down at Pentecost, Peter was filled, and he began to think like Jesus.

When Jesus delivers us from some sin or bad habit, He often makes us face the temptation again. But this time He gives us the power to come through it the right way. He gives impatient people the power to be patient. He gives hateful people the power to love. He gives fearful people courage.

Not only does He change our way of thinking, but He gives us a different reason for acting. When Don was asked to play his trumpet for church, he may have been afraid that he would be proud. Because Don was used to playing and feeling proud of himself for his skill. But when Don began playing for Jesus, he found that Jesus gave him an entirely different feeling. He was playing because he was grateful to Jesus for changing his life and giving him peace and forgiving his sins.

In some of us, the drive to create is so strong that we may fail to remember that we must let God direct what we create. We may develop a talent simply because it satisfies something deep inside ourselves to be able to do it. Or we may work hard to perfect a certain ability because it will make us feel that we are a little better than the next person.

Alan had a talent for singing. When he was three, he sang, "I'm a Little Teapot." With vibrato. When he finished a serious rendition of that, he turned to his mother and said, "Mamma, do I sound like an organ?" Alan's mother recognized that his keen musical ear had picked up the vibrato sound from the organ at church and that he might be musically gifted. So they began to practice singing. Although he was very shy about getting up in front, by the time he was ten, he finally sang a solo in the school play. He did very well and was asked to sing for church.

Alan was a little scared. But the church he attended was a small one, and he overcame his fear and sang. His parents sent a tape of his solo to his grandmother, and nothing would do then, but that Alan should go to his grandparents' church and sing there.

Alan at first consented, but as the time drew near for him to sing, he began to be afraid. His grandmother's church had a membership of 600. On the day Alan was supposed to sing, he panicked and refused.

Of course, his grandmother was very disappointed. Everyone tried to talk Alan into singing. But the more they talked, the more he balked. He would not do it.

Sabbath School started, and Alan breathed a sigh of relief. Now the pressure was off. Just then, one of the deacons—a man who had been a friend of the family for a long time—came to Alan. "Alan," he said kindly, "if you'll sing, I'll give you a dollar."

Something about the man's suggestion didn't feel right to Alan. He shook his head. No. The deacon said, "Come on, Alan. You've got a real good voice. Tell you what. If you sing, I'll give you two dollars."

Alan wavered. He didn't get money very often, and he could think of a lot of things two dollars would buy. And it really would please his grandmother. Then he felt that strange warning feeling again, and he said, firmly, "No, I don't want to sing."

Unknown to the deacon, Aunt Mary had been sitting close by and heard the conversation. Her lips pressed together with disapproval, until Alan said, "No, I don't want to sing." Then she smiled. After church she went to Alan and said quietly, "I'm proud of you, Alan. You passed the test."

"What did Aunt Mary mean, Mom?" Alan asked later, when he had told his mother what happened.

"There's only one reason to sing for church, Alan," said Mother. "Do you know what it is?"

"Because you're singing for Jesus?"

"That's right," said Mother. "If you don't feel like singing for Jesus, don't sing. Don't sing for money or for grandmother's approval or because singing is fun. Just sing for Jesus, Alan, always. That's the right reason to sing."

The Bible says, "Whether therefore ye eat, or drink, or whatsoever ye do, do all to the glory of God." 1 Corinthians 10:31.

But What If I Do Something Dumb?

Probably the hardest thing for a teenager to handle is doing just the wrong thing in front of his friends. It's embarrassing enough to make mistakes when he's alone, but when someone is there, it's a lot worse. It helps just a little bit to know that every single person in the world has also made a ridiculous mistake. But it usually doesn't help in time. On the other hand, you have to remember that embarrassment is a kind of teacher. After all, we wouldn't want to keep on doing the wrong kinds of things. It's good to want your friends to think you are a nice person. And embarrassment over mistakes helps us to remember not to make those same mistakes again.

On the other hand, it's not good to feel so awful about a mistake that you pull in the nice personality God gave you and go around ashamed of yourself. So sometimes we have to do a little "inside work" after something like that happens. The one thing you don't want to do is to let a hurt place just hurt. The reason it hurts is because some damage has been done. And it's not good first aid for the soul to tell it, "Oh, be quiet!" when it's damaged. It needs help.

The first kind of help it needs is to be thought about. Ask yourself just exactly what happened. And why did it happen? Now honestly, is it really serious? Is it something that I might be able to laugh about if I didn't keep on feeling sorry for myself?

All kinds of silly things happen to people. When I was in college, I got very worked up about something and pounded the table for emphasis. Unfortunately, it was the dinner table. And, unfortunately, I happened to hit the handle of my fork. The other end of the fork was buried in the mashed potatoes. Glop! The potatoes hit me right in the neck! And there was my boyfriend, sitting with four other people, watching the show!

You think that was bad? I cleaned the potatoes off with a napkin, swallowed my pride with a grin, and began my speech over. At the same point in the sentence, I again pounded my fist on the table, again hit the fork handle, and again flung mashed potatoes at my neck! *Encore!* This time they really laughed, and I decided that whatever point I was trying to make was backfiring. I was terribly embarrassed, but my accidents at the dinner table didn't seem to affect anyone else very seriously. In fact, I was chagrined to notice that it even appeared to brighten their day!

Some things, of course, aren't going to be laughable. But by all means, if they are, make the most of it! And if they aren't, cry. Or be righteously indignant. Or feel sorry for the other person. But when you're all through doing that, just think things out. Talk to God about it. Decide how you're going to feel about this incident. You must choose how to feel. Don't let your feelings take over and run the way you think—that's backwards. Your mind is the power that should be in charge, not your feelings. You choose a good way to look at your difficulty, and then Jesus will help you feel right about it.

But what if the thing that happened to you was really bad? There is no way you can laugh at it or reason it out. And what if it happened a long time ago?

He Is the God of Time

Most of the fences Satan has put up around our inner selves got put there because in the past something bad happened to us that made us afraid or angry or very sad. And people can't do anything about the past. Or can they?

Can they? What about God? Do you think God can do something about what happened to you six months ago or last year or even when you were born?

Picture a string laid out on the ground.

Now picture an ant walking along that string. And now let us suppose the ant doesn't like the way the string is laid out.

Too bad, ant!

We're like that ant. The string is like time. We have to walk along the course of our lives pretty much the way it's laid out for us. Especially when we're young, we can't do too much about the various twists and turns the string may take.

Now picture a boy coming along. He sees the ant walking along the string. He knows the ant doesn't like the way the string is laid out. And he is much bigger and stronger and wiser than the ant. He feels so sorry for the ant, that he just picks up the end of the string and straightens it out.

That's what God can do for us.

God is so much more powerful than we are, that He can easily do things with time that we can't do. He is the God of time. And wherever God goes in time, He takes love and healing with Him. The Bible tells us that His character is "merciful and gracious, longsuffering, and abundant in goodness and truth."

Doesn't that sound good? Say it out loud—"Merciful and gracious, longsuffering, and abundant in goodness and truth." That's what Jesus takes with Him when He goes into your past, back to some memory that is troubling you. *It doesn't matter how bad the memory is; Jesus can take away the pain.*

I was talking to a pretty dark-eyed teenager at one of our academies. She said, "I lay awake till 4 o'clock this morning, thinking about what my father did to me." She didn't say what her father had done, but I could tell it must've been serious to keep her awake most of the night. She had dark circles under her eyes and looked nervous and pale.

I said, "You should ask Jesus to touch that memory—He can heal it."

She said, "Oh, maybe He can heal some things, but this is so awful. I know He can't do anything about it."

"Have you tried?"

"No."

"Try it. Just say, 'Jesus, this is a terrible memory. I'd like to forget it, but I can't. Please come in and bring Your love along and make this sore place well.' It might take a little time, but He'll do it."

She looked doubtful, but finally she said that she would try.

As you begin to claim promises for yourself and find yourself feeling fearful or sad or upset about something that happened to you in the past, you can take the promise found in Isaiah 53:4, 5 to God, and ask Him to give it to you. Those verses say that Jesus has "borne our griefs, and carried our sorrows; . . . and with his stripes we are healed." These words tell us that not only are we healed from our *sins*, but also we can be healed of our *inside hurts*.

One time I was claiming this promise with my friend Diane, because Diane had a very painful memory. When she was a teenager, she was riding her bike home and had a flat tire. She was so very tired, but she knew she must change and repair that tire. There was no other way for her to get home. Wearily she got off her bike and took out the repair kit. Just as she started the repair, a mean boy came up to her. Instead of offering to help her fix the tire, as she hoped he would, he began to talk in a very filthy way. Poor Diane! She couldn't get away, and he wouldn't stop talking. So she was forced to listen to all the things he was saying. Because Diane was a good girl, this hurt her heart very much.

Before I prayed with Diane, I told her, "You just close your eyes and think about what happened, and Jesus will help you." So while I prayed, Diane remembered how she was riding her bike home. She thought of how she had the flat tire and how weary she was. She remembered how she started to change the tire and how the boy had come up and begun saying nasty things to her.

But then something different happened! In her imagination Diane saw Somebody coming down the road, walking fast. This Person came right up to them, and He looked stern. Before Diane could be afraid, He pointed at the boy and said, "Go!" The terrified boy turned and ran as fast as he could! Then the kind Man, whom Diane knew was Jesus, put His arm around her and said gently, "Here, let Me take care of that." And He fixed her bicycle tire!

As the boy in the beginning illustration picked up the string and changed it around, so Jesus had gone back in time, into Diane's memories, and changed them. He wrote a new ending to the story. Diane says that every time she thinks of the incident now, she can't help smiling and praising the Lord!

If you feel the need for Jesus to heal a memory from your past, you can be sure that He will. Maybe you won't have the same kind of experience Diane had. Some kinds of memories take a little more time to heal. But the promise that Jesus has borne our griefs and sorrows is just as sure, whether He decides to work very quickly or a little more slowly.

You know, Jesus didn't just promise to help us for this moment. He promised to help us and to be with us always. Sometimes when we read that promise in Matthew 28:20, we think, "I'm glad Jesus is going to be with me during the time of trouble just ahead." But for some of us the time of trouble we've already lived through is a lot more disturbing right now than the one we may face in the future. We don't realize that *always* doesn't only mean "in the future." It means "in the now" and "in the past" too. For the God of time is "the same yesterday, and to day, and for ever." Hebrews 13:8.

Some People Have Already Tried It

Before Jesus left earth, He prayed a beautiful prayer for His disciples. In that prayer, which you will find in John 17, He included not only Peter, James, John, and the rest of the Twelve who were with Him so often, but all those who "shall believe on me through their word." Verse 20. Not through Jesus' word, but through the disciples' word. They were supposed to tell others what Jesus had done for them, and others were to believe and become Christians—because of the disciples' words.

Considering that, it doesn't seem as if this book could be complete without including some of the things Jesus has done for others when they asked Him for help in releasing their Real Selves. Read on, then, about what happened to Linda, Frank, Jill, and Melody. And let faith and trust develop by listening to their words of witness for Jesus.

Linda was a young houswife with a tiny baby. She was a rather ordinary housewife, except for one thing. Linda was afraid. Not just easily startled, not only cautious, not merely a worrier, as young mothers sometimes are, but terribly, horribly afraid. She was ruled by fear. Linda was afraid to walk from the kitchen to the living room because—well, just because. And she was afraid to open the door when she wanted to go outside, because— And she was afraid to walk outdoors unless her husband or someone else was with her. At night when the baby cried, she was afraid to get out of bed in the dark and walk to its crib. She was afraid of rain, thunder, swimming, animals, and people who didn't believe as she did. The strange thing was that Linda didn't really realize anything was wrong. Perhaps she thought many other people were like that too. But one day she was reading in her Bible and came to Revelation 21:7, 8. It said, "He that overcometh shall inherit all things; . . . but the fearful, and unbelieving, and the abominable, and murderers . . . shall have their part in the lake which burneth with fire." She stopped reading with her finger on the word *fearful*. A sudden realization hit her. Just that morning, she had had to leave the living room and walk to the bathroom, and she remembered the fear that had come over her. By the time she arrived at the bathroom, she was shaking, her heart pounding fiercely, and sweat standing out on her forehead. She looked again at the verse. It said that the fearful were in the same group as the unbelieving, murderers, idolators, and liars! It dawned on her that something was wrong.

Linda called her friend Jan, told her what she had found, and asked Jan to come pray with her about it. That evening Jan arrived with her Bible, and Linda was so afraid of what might happen if they prayed that Jan had a hard time convincing her to pray! You have probably realized by now that Linda had more than just an ordinary fear. Jan realized that too. She felt that Satan was harrassing Linda. So she prayed a prayer that called on God to release Linda from her fear. She told Satan that Linda was God's child, and he had no right to make her afraid. Then she read a promise or two from the Bible. "For God hath not given us the spirit of fear; but of power, and of love, and of a sound mind." 2 Timothy 1:7. She read, "There is no fear in love; but perfect love casteth out fear." 1 John 4:18. Linda sat clutching her Bible and shaking. But as Jan prayed, she began to relax. Within a few minutes, all her fear was gone! From that moment to this, Linda has never been bothered by unreasonable fears. She learned to swim. They now have a big collie dog. She stands at the window now during thunderstorms and says to her children, "See the pretty lightning."

Jesus set Linda free from fear.

Frank was a convict. He was also a convert! During his stay in prison, he had let Jesus come into his life. Now he was a Christian. But he still smoked. Frank put every effort toward stopping this habit, but the best he could do was to get down to two cigarettes a day. Of course, two cigarettes a day are not as bad for a person as thirty cigarettes (a pack and a half) a day, but Frank wasn't satisfied with almost quitting. He knew he couldn't be baptized into the Seventh-day Adventist Church as long as he smoked even one cigarette. For weeks he prayed and tried, and tried and prayed. Sometimes he would go for a whole day, or even for two days, without smoking. Then he would smoke twenty cigarettes the next day to make up for it! It was so discouraging that he was ready to quit trying. One night he got down on his knees and said, "Lord, this is as far as I can go. I can quit all my cigarettes but two. But I can't quit the last two. If I ever overcome this habit, You'll have to quit the last two for me." Frank was just a new Christian. He didn't realize it then, but he had finally found the key to quitting. The Bible tells us that when Jesus died, our sins were nailed to the cross with Him. Of course, that doesn't do us any good unless we believe it and accept it into our lives. But when Frank told Jesus that He would have to quit for him, Frank discovered the rule for overcoming any kind of sin. Long ago, Frank's last two cigarettes had been nailed to the cross. Jesus had gotten the victory over Frank's smoking habit. When Frank accepted that, Jesus gave that victory to him. Frank never smoked again.

Jesus had given Frank victory.

Jill was only three or four years old when it happened. She and her mother and father were walking across the Golden Gate Bridge. They did that now and then, if the weather was fine. Jill was always just a little afraid to be up so high over the water, so she always held onto her parents' hands. One day, an especially beautiful one, they all stopped about half-way across the bridge to watch the sailboats scudding across the waves far below. They leaned on the rail, and Jill's mother relaxed and let go of Jill's hand. Her father picked Jill up so she could see over the rail. Then, in a teasing way, he held her out a little over the edge and said, "Whoops!" and pretended to let her fall. Jill screamed.

Her mother was angry. She said, "What are you trying to do? Scare her to death? Don't do that!"

In surprise, her father answered, "Why, I was just joking. You know I wasn't going to drop her!"

Then they each took Jill's hand again and walked the rest of the way across the bridge. Her parents forgot all about this incident, but Jill never did. She had nightmares about falling from high places, and every time she thought of almost being dropped over the Golden Gate Bridge, she felt awful and torn up inside. For years and years, this one small incident bothered Jill. It made her fearful of other things and caused her to be shy around strangers. And until she was thirty-six years old, Jill had nightmares about falling. That's a long time to carry a fear, isn't it?

Then one day Jill found out that we don't have to carry our old fears around with us forever—Jesus will take them away. That was good news to Jill. Although she had been a Christian all her life, Jill had never realized that Jesus can do away with fears from the past. She had thought they were part of the "cross" she had to carry in this life. The first thing Jill asked Jesus to heal was this memory of almost being dropped over the bridge.

The first day she prayed about it nothing happened. She still was terribly uncomfortable when she thought of it. The next day nothing happened either. At least, nothing Jill could identify. But she kept praying about it day after day. She let her imagination picture Jesus in the scene. She saw that He had been holding onto her all the time and that the angels had been there protecting her. So she kept praying, because even knowing all that, she was still afraid! You see, this was thirty-three-year-old fear, and fears that old are sometimes hard to let go of. It took three months for Jill's memory to be healed. Every day her picture of Jesus grew stronger and her memory of the fear became weaker. And one day she gave it to Jesus for the last time, and that was the end of it. That memory never did bother Jill again. She still remembers exactly what happened that warm spring day when she was so young. Oh, yes. But it doesn't trouble her any longer.

Jesus healed Jill's memory.

Melody was a sweet little girl with blue eyes, freckles, and two pigtails that her mother tied up in loops with big ribbons when Melody went to school. All dressed up in her plaid school dress, knee socks, and brown school shoes, she looked very neat and clean. Mother always told her she was a real "old-fashioned girl." Melody thought that must be a nice thing to be, since it pleased Mother. So she would smile and pretend to be walking through the woods to her one-room schoolhouse made of logs. Actually, she was walking along the sidewalk to the church school in the basement of the church, but Melody was a good pretender!

When Melody was a teenager, she met a really nice family. They were talented, good-looking, and fun to be with. They weren't as sold on "old-fashioned girls" as her mother had been, but they liked to do things naturally and didn't believe in dressing up a lot. After Melody had been around them for a while, she began to wear jeans more than plaid dresses. And she let her hair grow long and put it in two ponytails. "That's neat!" her new friends said. "You look just like a little cowgirl!" So Melody changed a bit to fit what these friends liked. It seemed to suit her pretty well.

Later still, Melody got married. Her husband hardly knew what an "old-fashioned girl" was like, and he wasn't much of a blue-jeans man himself. Instead of jeans, he liked a dress on his wife. And, mainly, he wanted a woman who could control herself. He didn't think a whole lot of hysterical women who scream and get all excited about every little thing. So Melody changed again. She began to wear housedresses, and one day her mother was very surprised to be greeted with, "Oh, hi, Mom," instead of the usual shriek of surprise and delight that Melody gave when Mother came to visit. But Melody was trying to control herself, and that pleased her husband very much indeed.

About the time Melody was thirty years old, things had come to such a pass that she found herself sitting on the hillside in the pasture with a pen and tablet writing, "Who am I, anyway?"

She decided that people weren't a very reliable source of reference for that question. She felt that if she ever was to find out what she was like deep down inside, she had better ask God. And He told her. In fact, He's never quit! Melody knows herself better every day. What came out of Melody was not an old-fashioned girl, or a cowgirl, or a self-controlled, housedress-wearing housewife. What Melody became was a talented woman who excelled in the field of music. She's naturally rather serious, scarcely ever wears blue jeans, and is always delighted to see her mother. Everyone who knows her is much happier with Melody the way she is now, than they were with the way they thought she was. And God is happier too. Melody never was who her friends thought she was. When she tried to fit their image of her, things came out a mess for Melody. But when she let God show her what He had created her to be, the picture got all straightened out.

God gave Melody herself.

Dan told me that in trying to decide what he should be like, he just copied parts of other people that he liked and became that way himself. Dan isn't a Christian, you see, so he has to do things secondhand. A Christian can go straight to God and get the information he needs for whatever problem he has to solve. So, as Dan told me, "I'm part of about thirty different people. And I don't know who *I* really am." Until he finds out, I always think of him as "Dan, 30-X." It's a shame that a good-looking, six-foot-two, intelligent person like Dan hasn't found himself yet. Do you know anyone like that?

Jesus did big things for Linda—and Frank and Jill and Melody and _____. That blank is for your

66

name, because He will do all these things, and much more, for you too. He's aching to do it. He died to do it! He wants to take care of the fears and hurts and sins and bad memories and twisted personalities—so the Real Me—or the Real You—can stand up.

The Gospel According to You—The Real You!

Do you realize that the only records we have of Jesus' life were not written by Jesus? They were written by His friends.

One Gospel record was written by a Son of Thunder, whose Real Self turned out to be so gentle and sweet that he still is known as John the Beloved. Another record was written by a well-known cheat, whose Real Self, released by Jesus, came out as a sacrificing missionary—Matthew. There is no evidence that the Gospel writer Luke ever saw Jesus personally. He wrote the reports he had heard from the disciples. His Gospel demonstrates that you don't have to have seen Jesus in the flesh in order to know Him personally.

The power of these men's witness was in the fact that *they had been trapped in sin*, behind the barriers of bad behavior and guilt, *and Jesus set them free*.

What is the good news according to you? Did you know that you, too, are giving a record to the world, yes, to the whole universe, of what Jesus is really like?

When a shy person responds to Jesus by becoming open and friendly, when an unclean person becomes pure, when a hateful person turns loving, the story of Jesus is told all over again. It's not only by our words that we witness.

Sometimes we get the impression that witnessing is one of those rather boring Christian duties that is expected of us as church members. We visualize ourselves going from door to door in our town or neighborhood, repeating the speech we learned at the last witnessing class on how to lead your neighbor to Christ.

Nothing could be farther from the truth. Witnessing is living! Living is witnessing. Whichever way you want to put it, it means the same. There is a time, true, for door-to-door work. But that is only a small part of our total witness.

Once you understand how good life is with Jesus in you, you just can't help wanting to help others experience it too. Your hands, your voice, your choices are all controlled by the Holy Spirit who dwells in your mind. And all those qualities have an influence on others. Sooner or later, you'll notice someone who has the same barriers you used to have, and you'll want to show him the way to freedom. Jesus is pleased that you do that, for He told us to "loose the bands of wickedness, to undo the heavy burdens, and to let the oppressed go free." Isaiah 58:6. It is interesting to note that about the only thing Jesus said concerning the way people dress was that if we see someone without a coat, we're to give him one of ours. He seems to have failed to say much about our correcting the hairstyles of others, also. Although Paul gives us the standards of dress for Christians, he refuses to tell us how we must interpret those standards and impose them on others. We are our brother's—and sister's—keepers, but our part is to bring the person into contact with God; God's part is to bring about the changes.

In fact, Jesus has gone through great pains to make sure that we do not let the outside appearance of a person influence us unduly. He has gone so far as to give us a gift of the Holy Spirit called "discernment"—to help us help others correctly.

Suppose there's a girl at school who comes from a non-Christian home. She wears a lot of makeup and ultra-trendy clothes, and she tries to copy the latest hairstyles she sees on the TV stars. With *discernment*, you see that this girl is not really as interested in the styles as she is in looking nice. You see that she depends on her friends' opinions to gauge her own value. But that *desire to look nice* is her special gift from Jesus. Jesus likes things to look nice too. We may interpret "Behold, I make all things new" (Revelation 21:5) as indicating God's approval of beautiful appearance.

But with *discernment*, you will not be as concerned about how this girl *looks* as about how she *feels*. When she knows Jesus and chooses Him as her ruling Spirit, she'll start dressing, talking, and acting differently, without your having to say much about her habits. Your part is to show her a little of what Jesus is like— by your kindness to her, by failing to get angry if she irritates you, by sticking up for her when others try to put her down—so she'll want to choose Him too.

Perhaps there's a boy at school who bullies the smaller children. With *discernment*, you understand that inside he feels helpless and perhaps even afraid. He may be angry because of something he cannot control. Perhaps he has a bad homelife or can't get through his studies very well. His bad behavior is a way of showing how frustrated he is. *Look for his special gifts from Jesus!* Maybe he is physically strong and good at putting things together with his hands. Jesus was that way. He had to be strong physically and skillful to be a carpenter in those times. When you see this, you will know that instead of returning anger, you must return love. Jesus said "Do good to them that hate you, and pray for them which despitefully use you." Matthew 5:44. When this boy understands how God's love shows itself through human beings (that's *you*), he'll become a defender of those smaller than himself.

Ask Jesus to give you discernment so you will know how to help others. It's true that people have walls and fences and barriers around their Real Selves. But the way to break them down is not with the sledgehammer of attack or the grindstone of nagging or a D-8 Caterpillar of control and accusation. We don't have to use heavy equipment to break down the walls of fear, shyness, anger, hatred, and the rest. There's a much faster and better way.

They melt!

They melt in the Son-shine of God's love that is shining out from your free, loving, sweet, original personality. It's called "*Christ in you*, the hope of glory." Colossians 1:27, italics supplied.

Catching the Picture

Even if you faithfully follow all the directions in this book and understand everything written here so far, you will still fall short of feeling whole and complete—unless you have "caught the picture."

Have you ever seen one of those double-exposure photographs that are in style right now? Usually there's a front view of the person, and superimposed over that, either a side view or a close-up of the face. That's the kind of picture I'd like to catch right now—a double exposure of you and Jesus. Close your eyes and imagine it.

Right out in front is you, of course. That's the first thing people will see. But superimposed over you is a view of Jesus. It almost looks as if He's in the background, but if you study the picture more closely, you'll see He's actually in front. The picture of you is good—but what really makes this photograph is *the image of God*.

And I'd like you to try to catch something that even a good double exposure of you and Jesus couldn't catch. You see, it's not just Jesus *and* you; it's Jesus *in* you. Jesus in the tone of your voice, in the look from your eyes, in the gentleness of your hands, in the clarity of your thoughts. It's His mind, *in you*.

Touch this picture carefully, for it is the greatest of miracles.

When Jesus came to this earth, He took on a man's body with all its weaknesses. But He never took man's sinful thoughts. Jesus' mind was the same kind of mind Adam had before he sinned. It had power to choose to do right and obey. It also had the possibility of doing wrong, just as Adam did. Because Jesus kept in close connection with His Father, His mind always chose to obey.

Now He offers this same possibility to us. If we will accept Him as our Saviour and keep in close connection with Him, He will make it possible for us to obey as He did. If we let His perfect mind rule ours, we will speak, think, talk, and act like Him.

Don't fool yourselves into thinking that you can do what you please. Either you will be under the control of Jesus, or you will be under the control of the enemy, Satan. *You must choose. Not to choose, is to allow Satan to control.* And what a sad double exposure our lives are when the figure of Satan is superimposed over ourselves.

When you picture yourself and Jesus as one, picture yourself complete. For even though it takes time for Jesus to break down the barriers that Satan may have erected in our lives, when we choose Him we are counted as perfect.

That idea may trouble you, for you have probably found out by now that nothing you can do will ever qualify for the label "perfect." But Jesus has promised that if we choose Him and give our best in loving obedience to Him, He will lay a gentle covering over us. The gentle covering is His own robe of perfection. It's called the robe of righteousness. When God looks down upon us, He sees the gentle covering that His Son has spread over us, and He recognizes it as His

Son's robe. Anyone covered with the Son's robe is counted as perfect in the books of heaven.

Under the gentle covering of His own perfection, Jesus does His work on our hearts. The covering protects us from Satan; it encourages us; it wraps us in peace and love. It also gives us power to obey. We are foolish to deliberately come out from under the covering by choosing to disobey, for then we are again on Satan's territory. That is what Adam did. Only if we choose to disobey do we come out from under the robe of Christ's righteousness.

When we make mistakes, we can know that Jesus will correct us and defend us against the enemy. When we gain victories over our problems, we know that it was Jesus who did it in us. The longer one lives under the gentle covering, the more one knows how weak he is and how strong God is. And wonderfully, that brings a great peace.

When I think of this, I remember Frankie.

He was almost too old for special-education, but he'd never been in school before. A concerned social worker had found Frankie tied to the bed in his bedroom. The place was filthy—Frankie was denied bathroom privileges. He was very thin. When his parents remembered, they threw his food in on the floor, and there was never enough for the growing boy. From this nightmare existence, Frankie was put in the home of the special-education teacher, Miss Sally.

Miss Sally treated Frankie tenderly and lovingly. This was the first time he had ever known love, and Frankie responded eagerly. He was thirsty for affection, hungry for attention. And he got it from Miss Sally. When he felt well enough, Miss Sally took him to school. And that is where I saw him for the first time. It was obvious from the start that Frankie would do anything to please Miss Sally.

So now Frankie stared intently through his glasses at the money spread before him on the desk.

"OK, Frankie," said the teacher patiently, "what kind of coin is this?"

Frankie looked hard at the coin and after a long pause said, "Penny."

"Good, Frankie! You're right. Now what kind of coin is this?

"Nickel." said the boy.

"That's right, Frankie! You're doing real well. Now here's a difficult one. What is this?"

Frankie looked hard at the small silver coin. He thought and thought. He broke out in perspiration, for he wanted so badly to please the teacher with the correct answer. What if he were wrong? He wasn't as smart as the other boys and girls, and he had never heard some of these words before. He thought it was— no, maybe not— His thoughts seemed to go round and round. Miss Sally sat quietly holding the small silver piece.

"Dime," Frankie said hoarsley.

Miss Sally put her arms around Frankie and kissed him. "Frankie, you did it! You remembered the dime! Oh, Frankie, today you are going to get a great big 100 beside your name!"

And as she drew the beautiful, bright red 100 on his paper, fourteen-year-old Frankie began to cry. It was the first 100 he had ever received.

That's how Jesus does with us. He has rescued us from sin and a bad kind of life. He patiently loves us and teaches us how to be. Maybe some of us aren't as smart as others. Maybe some of us don't have big talents. But under the gentle covering of His love and goodness, He helps us along. And if we do our best, in His book we get a big, beautiful "Perfect."

With Jesus we score 100. Without Him, we score 0.

With Jesus we overcome. Without Him, we're slaves to bad habits.

With Jesus we're saved. Without Him, we're lost.

With Him, we're at peace, free to enjoy being ourselves. Without Him, we're blocked and frustrated behind the barries of fear, guilt, and sin.

The choice we have to make really isn't very hard, is it?

Are you willing to go with Jesus, so the Real You can stand up and show the universe a little of what God is like?

Promises for Personality Problems

Disbelief

Titus 1:2. A faith and knowledge resting on the hope of eternal life, which God, who does not lie, promised before the beginning of time.

Desire to be saved

John 3:16. For God so loved the world that he gave his one and only Son, that whosoever believes in him shall not perish but have eternal life.

Guilt and condemnation

John 3:17. For God did not send his Son into the world to condemn the world, but to save the world through him.

Lack of understanding God

1 John 5:20. We know also that the Son of God has come and has given us understanding, so that we may know him who is true. And we are in him who is true—even in his Son Jesus Christ. He is the true God and eternal life.

Any kind of sin

1 John 1:9. If we confess our sins, he is faithful and just and will forgive us our sins, and purify us from all unrighteousness.

Aloneness, dismay, weakness	**Isaiah 41:10.** So do not fear, for I am with you; do not be dismayed, for I am your God. I will strengthen you and help you; I will uphold you with my righteous right hand.
Any need	**Psalm 84:11.** For the Lord is a sun and shield; the Lord bestows favor and honor; no good thing does he withhold from those whose walk is blameless.
Lack of wisdom	**James 1:5.** If any of you lack wisdom, he should ask God, who gives generously to all without finding fault, and it will be given to him.
Unattractiveness	**Psalm 90:17.** May the favor [beauty] of the Lord our God rest upon us.
Fear, hate, weakness, weak mind	**2 Timothy 1:7.** For God did not give us a spirit of timidity, but a spirit of power, of love, and of self-discipline.
Any work of Satan	**1 John 3:8.** The reason the Son of God appeared was to destroy the devil's work.
Tormenting fear	**1 John 4:18.** There is no fear in love. But perfect love drives out fear, because fear has to do with punishment.

Grief, sor-
row, sin

Isaiah 53:4, 5. Surely he took up our in-firmities and carried our sorrows. . . . He was pierced for our transgressions, . . . crushed for our iniquities; the punishment that brought us peace was upon him, and by his wounds we are healed.

If you believe and trust in Him and are willing to do things His way, after you have reviewed the four steps on page 42, open your Bible to the promise you have chosen. Then, remembering that Jesus is kind and loving and doesn't condemn us, read the promise that you need. Put your hand over it. Now close your eyes and think about Jesus giving you what you have asked for.

If you have a problem that is really big—and you find yourself shivering or perspiring or feeling a little sick to your stomach or getting a headache—Satan is trying to get you to give up. But you can have the protection of Jesus by saying out loud, "I ask that the blood of Jesus cover me." That means you are appealing to God the Father to protect you. When Jesus died (shed His blood), He paid for your protection from Satan. Read your promise out loud and tell Jesus you believe it, even though you might not be feeling too well right then. He will help you. He will protect you and give you what you need.